Introdu

Science is life, biochemistry, physics

It is a summary of life and life is wonderful, exciting and exciting

Also, these sciences are amazing and wonderful

Unforfunately, we study it in a dry, semi-theoretical manner

Until the problem became problems and became an example in difficulty

If you cannot understand anything

Find someone to tell you (is chemistry means)

The subject, which I hope will be renewed, God willing

Directed to every mother looking for modern means to deliver knowledge to her children

Combined with fun to learn

Likewise, for every male and female teacher who is saved in his work

And searches for a way to endear his students in the scientific subject

Without costing him so much in light of the near-no possibilities

In government schools and also directed to all science lovers

The topic aims to simplify science and provides a set of scientific experiments

Photographer, which can be done with tools and materials, most of which are available at home

With a very simple explanation of the scientific base on which the experience was built

I wish fun and benefit to everyone who passes the topic

Content

The eruptive volcano experience

Experience the testing of different flavors Sense of taste Sweet - sour - salted – bitter

Crystallised Candy
Diet Coke and Mentos Experiment

Candy Science Experiment Supplies

Hurricane experience inside a bottle

Experience a rainbow in a glass cup

Pasta missile

Hand-made lava lamp

Immediate ice

Iron magnetized liquid

Baking soda volcano

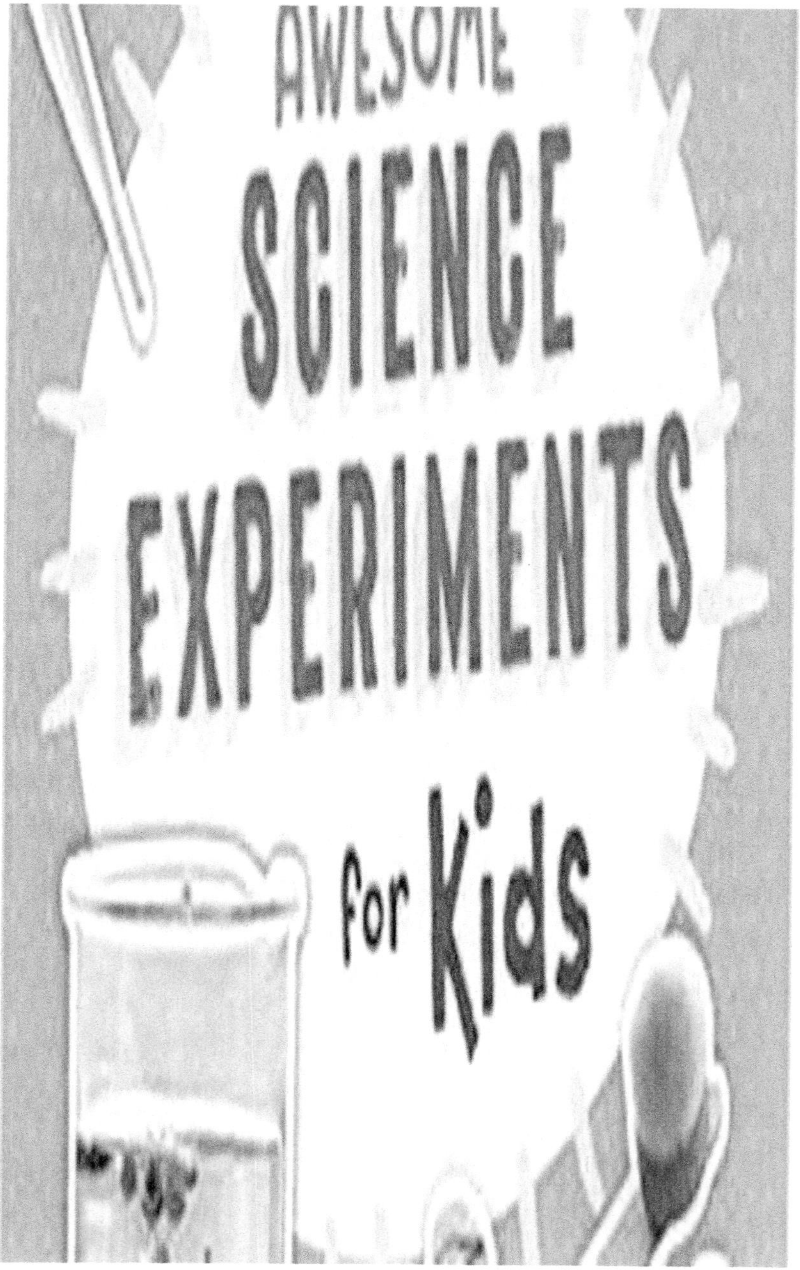
AWESOME
SCIENCE
EXPERIMENTS
for Kids

Egg shell stripping experience

Required tools

An egg

Wide jar with lid

White vinegar

The steps

Gently place the egg inside the jar

Put the white vinegar until the egg is submerged, the egg will float at first and

But then it will sink down

After a few moments, the patches will start to appear due to the rise of carbon dioxide on the surface of the egg shell

Close the cap and lay the egg like this for a week

After a week, gently remove the egg, and then wash it under water. The shell will be removed

Easily if not, easily put it back on vinegar another day

Now the egg is made without the outer shell, you can now enjoy its appearance in front of sunlight and feel its soft texture

Experiment analysis

This experiment is a classic reaction to a citrus reaction, where vinegar contains acetic acid and eggs containing calcium carbonate.

The calcium carbonate in the eggshell interacts with the acetic acid in the vinegar to form a compound dissolved in water, which is calcium acetate, and carbon dioxide gas. This reaction dissolves the egg shell but maintains the inner part of the egg, making the eggs naked without the outer shell

Experience: How can you blow the balloon with sodium bicarbonate and vinegar?

The right age for the experience

From 4 years to 8 years old

The goal of the experiment

Students learn about gas and chemical reactions by discovering how to inflate a balloon with baking soda and vinegar

The aim of this project is to demonstrate the strength of the gas that is produced when you mix baking soda and vinegar, and the goal is that the balloon can be detonated by the gas created

Questions of activity that should be directed to the child

What do you think will happen when we mix baking soda and vinegar (what will be produced)?

What do you think will happen to the balloon?

Why does the balloon stop blowing up (why doesn't the reaction stop)?

Crisis materials

Balloon 1 for each student

1 small bottle for each student

Small suppression 1 per student

Baking soda 2 tablespoons per student

Vinegar 4 ounces per student

Experience

Using funnel, add baking soda to each balloon

Pour the vinegar into a bottle

Carefully install the balloon over an open bottle, and be careful not to drop the baking soda into the vinegar

When the balloon is comfortably attached to the bottle mouth, allow baking soda to fall into the vinegar.

Watch the chemical reaction and effect on the balloon and then record your notes

It is preferable to do the experiment in the presence of an adult supervisor with the child

Three different balloon experiments

Balloon nails first experiment

__Tools__: 2 balloons - desk pins

<u>Experience</u>

Blow the balloon

Place the balloon over one nail

What will happen?

Of course the balloon will explode

Blow up another balloon

Put a lot of pins and then place the balloon on top of them

What will happen to the balloon this time?

Nothing will happen because the pressure is equal on all the pins and not the same as the previous time on one balloon

The second experience

Tools: balloon - empty plastic bottle - sodium bicarbonate - white vinegar - funnel

Place soda bicarbonate into the balloon using the funnel

Then put the white vinegar inside the bottle

Place the balloon on the bottle and allow the sodium carbonate to descend into the bottle

Observe the reaction that will take place and how the carbon dioxide will come out as a result of the reaction that will inflate the balloon

The third experience

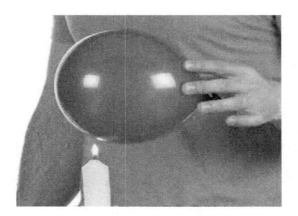

Tools:

2 water balloon candles

Candle light

Blow the balloon and place it close to the candle

Watch what will really happen as you thought the balloon had exploded

The balloon was re-inflated, but this time with water, not air, and closed tightly

Bring the balloon close to the candle

What will happen to the balloon?

Nothing happened because the water made the balloon cool inside

Alpha lamp experience

The right age for the experience

From the age of 5 years to 7 years

The goal of the experiment

To explore the relationship between oil and water in terms of density

To observe a chemical reaction between

acid and a base

Questions of activity that should be directed to the child

What happens when you add water to a plastic bottle? Why do you think this happened?

What happens when food colors are added to the bottle? Why do you think this happened?

What happens when you add sparkling to the bottle? Why do you think this happened?

Crisis materials

1 clean plastic soda bottle, with cap

Vegetable oil

Food color, macrocrome, or any kind of disinfectant

Water

Sparkling nettle or effervescent powder

Suppression

Experience

Place beneath you and under the materials used in the experiment, newspaper to keep the place used for the experiment clean

Fill a plastic bottle ¾ full of vegetable oil

Add water to the neck of the bottle, and leave a little space between the water line and the top of the container. (You can always add more water later

Make a decision about the desired color for the lava lamp. Then choose this color from the food coloring list accordingly

Add 10 or more drops of food coloring to the bottle

Place the bubbler and watch for every reaction

When mixed, put a bottle cap

Shake the bottle back and forth and observe the reaction. Tip; shake the bottle in different directions. Observe the reactions then write down your feedback

Experiment with the floating egg

Tools

3 eggs

3 cups large empty water

Water 250 ml

Salt

Experience

I will fill the cups with water until halfway through equally

Then add 3 tablespoons of salt to only two of the three cups and wait

Until the salt is completely dissolved

Place the first egg in the third cup, with no salt, and you will see that the egg is completely submerged in the cup

Put the second egg in the second cup filled with the dates, you will see the egg remains on top

Place the third egg in the first cup, it will remain on top, then carefully add some water to this cup

What do you notice? Yes, the water became over the egg. This is because the density of water is lighter than the density of water to which salt is added, and you will see the egg stuck in the middle of the water

Tap Water

Salt Water

Make wonderful things from Sodium polyacrylate

First, magic colored snow

The necessary tools

A glass of glass

Food colors

Water

Sodium polyacrylate

You can get it from gardening tools stores or from inside diapers, as they are small salt-like balls inside the diaper

Experience

Put the water and the colors on it inside the cup or the glass jar

Mix them well

Sodium guest

Watch the magic of ice

Secondly, the rubber balls

The necessary tools

Glass

Water

Pinch of salt

Sodium polyacrylate

You can get it from gardening tools stores or from inside diapers, as they are small salt-like balls inside the diaper

Experience

Put sodium in a cup

Add water to it

Wait a few seconds

Then mix them well with salt

Wait a while for the balls to form

You can add food color to get colored balls

Do orange floats or drown?

The necessary tools:

An orange.

Deep bowl.

Water.

Steps:

Fill the bowl with water.

Put the orange in the water and see what happens.

Then peel the orange peel and repeat the experiment again. Watch what happens?

*what happens?

The first time you put an orange in a bowl of water floated to the surface but after removing the crust it sank to the bottom, why did this happen?

Because the orange peel is filled with small air pockets that help to give it less density of water, which made it float on the surface.

But by removing the orange peel (and all the pockets of air), the density of the orange increases, so it becomes higher than the water, which makes it drown.

What is the density?

It is the mass of an object in relation to a volume. Objects that contain a lot of mass in a certain size have a high density, while the same size of objects but small amounts of mass have a low density.

The experience of attracting colors

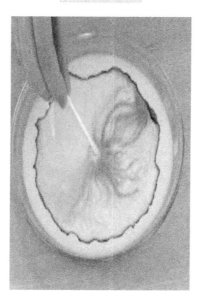

This experiment needs to have the following mentioned to start with: A flat, wide plastic dish. Liquid colors. Wood stick. Liquid Soap.

Steps of the experiment: A quantity of liquid colors is placed in the plastic plate in the form of round points. Dip the wood column tip into a liquid soap. The end of the wooden column is placed in the center of the plate between the color points. It can be seen that the colors are attracted to the soap on the edge of the wood stick.

How to create a volcano as a scientific experiment

The making of a traditional volcano

The necessary materials

An empty can of soft drink, or a clean glass jar.

Butter paper, large carton, or newspaper.

Amount of putty is enough to form the volcano's mountain around the can.

Three quarters of a cup of vinegar.

A few drops of red food stain.

Tablespoon of clear liquid.

A tablespoon and a half of baking soda

Manufacturing Method

Place the carton or butter paper over the table, then place the can in the middle and coat it with putty, forming a mountain with a nozzle, and set it aside for at least two hours to dry completely.

Mix the vinegar with 1 tablespoon of the clear liquid, stain and leave aside.

Put the baking soda in a paper napkin and close it with plastic rubber

To make the volcano erupt, pour the vinegar mixture into the crater, then drop the baking soda into it.

The volcano in the bottle

The necessary materials

A bottle of clean soft drink

Dough, paste, clay or tin foil to fill the bottle.

Half a cup of six percent oxygen water, i.e., twenty hydrogen peroxide, is available in cosmetic stores (higher levels of hydrogen water can be used for a more raging volcano.

Six drops of red food stain.

Two drops of yellow food stain

Two tablespoons of clear liquid.

Tablespoon of instant dry yeast.

Three tablespoons of water

Manufacture method

Because this method contains chemicals, it is recommended that an adult monitor the method of manufacture.

Place the bottle on newspaper, or any piece of large paper or cardboard.

Use the clay, or putty, to make a long, beautiful mountain around the bottle, leaving the nozzle without closing, and leave it in a place where there is an airway to dry completely.

Pour the oxygen water with a funnel into the bottle, then mix the clear liquid with food colorants and pour it into the bottle with the oxygen water.

Mix the yeast with water, then put it in the bottle and watch the eruptions.

Notes

It is preferable to conduct these experiments in a large and spacious place, or outside because of the chaos these experiments will cause.

In the first experiment, make sure the tissue is closed tightly.

Refer to a safe distance when conducting any type of scientific experiment.

Plastic is made from milk and white vinegar only

Required tools

A cup of warm milk, not boiled

4 tea spoon of white vinegar

Mixing bowl

Wooden stick for mixing

Colander

Napkin paper

The steps

Mix the vinegar and milk together well for a minute. You will see how the protein in the milk starts to break apart thanks to the acid in the vinegar.

Then, strain the mixture well

Place the solid over the tissue paper

It is possible to add drops of food color

Shape the material the way you want and then leave it for two days to become solid

Now your shape is ready you can decorate it with your room

Experience the speed of sound

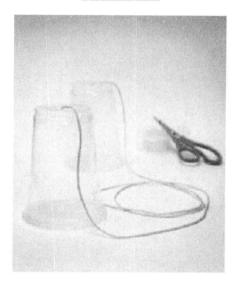

The right age for the experience

From the age of 5 years to 7 years

The goal of the experiment

Demonstrating the speed of sound transmission through the air and through the rope

Questions of activity that should be directed to the child

When you talk to a friend, your voices travel from your mouths through the air (gas) to each other's ears. What happens when you call mouths and ears to cut it from the rope?

Crisis materials

Two cups of paper or plastic you can use small yogurt containers

A pair of scissors

Rope

Sticky tape

Friend

Experience

Use the last point of the scissors to make a hole in the middle of the bottom of each cup. (Depending on your age, it may be best to be an adult doing this step

Have a friend stand a few feet away and talk to you in a normal voice, not shouting or loudly

Keep moving away until you don't hear each other

Hold one of the glasses in front of your mouth and talk to your friend as well. You are at the same far distance. Now can you hear each other? Cut a thread to stretch the distance between you and your friend when you were unable to hear each other

Paste both ends of the rope through the holes in the cup bottoms and the tape ends safe for these bottoms

Hold one cup and your friend holds the other, and move until the rope is tight and not flabby

Talk to one cup while your friend holds the other cup over her ear. (Remember to keep the cord tight) Switch.

Now can you hear each other through cups? (Remember to move the glasses from your mouths to your ears again and again depending on if you are listening or talking.) Why do you think attaching cups with a string allows you to hear each other?

More fun with this project! Try it with longer and longer pieces of thread. How far is the distance and the phone - the cup - is still working? What will happen if you use the different sizes, shapes, and materials of the mugs?

Luminous water experience

And make luminous things

from him

The necessary tools

Various highlighter pens

Sodium fluorescein

Glass cups

Water

Plastic cups

Plastic flowers or anything plastic you want to make it glow in the dark

Experimental

Empty the Hi-Lite pen content into the plastic cup

Mix each color in the water

Turn off the lights and watch

You got bright water

Soak the flower in any cup of bright water and see what happens after a few hours

The flower absorbed the water and became luminous

Soak anything in the luminous water for a few hours, and it will also become so

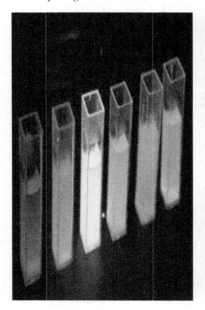

The eruptive volcano experience

Required tools

Hydrogen peroxide half a cup

One teaspoon of yeast

Hot water (approximately 2 tablespoons) in a small dish

Food colors

Dishwashing liquid

Empty bottle

Tray to stand the bottle on it

Suppression

The steps

Pour hydrogen peroxide into a bottle

Mix the yeast with hot water

Mix the washing liquid and food color into the hydrogen peroxide in a bottle

Yeast mixture is added to a bottle

Go back and get ready to spin

The scientific explanation

First, hydrogen peroxide breaks down into water and oxygen, and the enzymes in the yeast accelerate this reaction and then react

The washing liquid with oxygen makes this abundant foam, but the food color is only for fun and the wonderful view of the furan

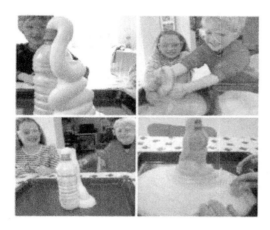

Experience the testing of different flavors

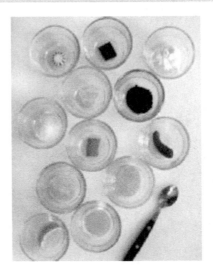

Sense of taste

Sweet - sour - salted – bitter

The right age for the experience

5-6 years

The goal of the experiment

It makes children able to tell the difference between the four flavors: sweet - sour - salted - bitter

Development and exploration of the sense of taste in the child

Questions of activity that should be directed to the child

Can you distinguish between the four flavors? Which of these flavors give the sweet taste...? Can you distinguish between different foods now?

Crisis materials

The amount of subjects varies according to the number of children participating in the activity

These are the suggested foods that can be replaced with the same properties if they are not available

12 small plates

One tablespoon of sugar

One number mint candy

One tablespoon of honey

One number lemon

One number pickled cucumber

One hanging yogurt

One tablespoon of salt

One number salted French fries

One tablespoon cheese

One number unsweetened chocolate

One tablespoon of coffee

One number grapefruit

Experience

Each component is placed in a dish

Place all dishes on one table

Taste the sugar; tell the child that this is a sweet taste

Lemon taste, mm. Tell the child that this is a sour taste

Taste the salt; tell the child that this is a salty taste

Taste unsweetened chocolate; tell the child that this is bitter

Now I make the child taste of the rest of the dishes to match the previous tastes and determine what kind of taste he tastes to discover more what is his sense of taste

Crystallised candy

You need: 2 glasses of water, 5 glasses of sugar, small wooden kebab sticks, some thick paper, some clear glasses, a saucepan, food colorings.

The experiment: Make some sugar syrup by adding a couple of teaspoons of ordinary sugar to a quarter glass of water. Sprinkle a piece of paper with some sugar. Dip the kebab sticks in the mixture, stirring them so that pieces of sugar start to stick to them. Make sure the mixture is spread evenly along the stick, and then lay them out on the paper.

Leave the sticks to dry out overnight. In the morning, dissolve five glasses of sugar in two glasses of water in a heated saucepan. Leave the resulting syrup to cool down for 15 minutes, although not for too long as otherwise the crystals won't form. Then pour it into some empty jars and add food coloring in different colours. Place the now-ready kebab sticks in the jars, but make sure they touch neither walls or bottom — use a clothes peg to do this.

Diet Coke and Mentos Experiment

How does the Diet Coke and Mentos experiment work?

The carbonation in the soda reacts with the Mentos candy and little carbon dioxide bubbles form all over the candies. This happens very quickly and when it's fast enough then an explosion occurs.

Mentos are the candy of choice because their surface is very porous and ideal for creating lots and lots of carbon dioxide bubbles. Any soda will work but the aspartame in diet sodas produce a bigger reaction because it lowers the surface tension of the soda.

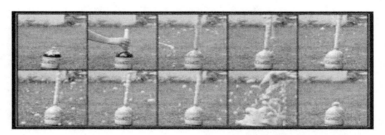

Candy Science Experiment Supplies

CONVERSATION HEART SCIENCE

Candy Science Experiment Supplies:

conversation hearts or other candy

Water

Vinegar

Honey (or other sugary substance)

Salt/salt water

Microwave or freezer

Bleach

The supplies can be easily switched for any item your kids want to test; these are just the ones my kids picked!

Basically we wanted to see what would happen to the conversation hearts as we added each item to them. The kids wrote or drew each item on their papers and predicting what they thought would happen.

We then added 1 item at a time (salt, honey, water, vinegar, salt water, etc) or put them in the freezer or microwave and recorded our observations.

The water dissolved the candy after awhile. The vinegar bubbled on some of the candies at first, but not others, until eventually it all bubbled up and dissolved. Honey didn't react and neither did microwaving or freezing–I was surprised about the microwave results!

The salt alone had no effect, but salt water did. A reader reported that adding bleach was very cool and pulled the sugars from the candies upward–we can't wait to try it

After we were done we talked about why we thought our predictions were correct or incorrect and looked for patterns in the results.

Candy science experiments are a great way to get kids to think like a scientist and practice their problem solving skills!

Hurricane experience inside a bottle

You can make your own tornado in a bottle, all you need is two bottles, a tube to connect them together, and some water.

When the liquid circulates in the upper bottle, it forms a vortex during its descent into the lower bottle, due to the inevitable rise of the air, while the water flows down into a cyclone-like formation, and some glossy materials, food colorings or lighting of the bottle can be added to make it look more beautiful.

Experience a rainbow in a glass cup

This experiment takes advantage of the density to create a rainbow inside a glass cup. When we add sugar to the liquid, the solution becomes more dense, and the more sugar you add the more the density of the solution, and if you made four solutions of different density and color, the colors will line up on layers on top of each other, so that the more dense solution sits Which contains more sugar at the bottom of the cup and the less dense settles to the top.

Pasta missile

Believe it or not, you can create a science experiment for a simple rocket motor using some yeast, hydrogen peroxide, a flask, fire and a piece of uncooked pasta. When the yeast is mixed with hydrogen peroxide they interact, producing pure oxygen gas, you just have to direct this gas through the pasta piece Hollows and then ignite it to get your missile

Hand-made lava lamp

Alka-seltzer pills are very effective in treating heartburn and stomach upset (pills consist of aspirin and citric acid known as lemon salt and sodium bicarbonate known as baking soda), but you probably do not know that it is good either if you want to make a lamp. Bath yourself.

The fact that water and oil possess two different densities and poles, when trying to mix them together they will always water down, which can be stained with food colorings to give it the desired color, Alka Seltzer grain powder interacts with water, creating air-laden water bubbles that explode at the surface and return down to the bottom, which is similar to what We see it in the lava lamp.

Immediate ice

In order for the water to freeze, it must have a nucleus that allows solid crystals to form (a nucleus here is the beginning of the formation of ice and it easily forms on impurities in the water).

Snow naturally consists of electrolytes and particles dissolved in water that allow this, but distilled water can reach temperatures below minus zero before it turns to ice.

When you put a bottle of distilled water in the refrigerator for about three hours, it will cool to a degree below the freezing point of normal water without freezing.

Iron magnetized liquid

This experiment will make seeing the real action of magnetic fields easy.

All you need is some iron oxide, some water and a glass bottle. When you put a strong magnet on the side of the bottle, the iron filings will pull toward it, piling up over it and follow the movement of the magnet as you move it.

Baking soda volcano

The chemical reaction in this experiment produces baking soda and vinegar lava that rushes outside the structure of a mini-volcano, as the chemical reaction between them produces carbon dioxide gas, which compresses and accumulates inside the plastic bottle hidden inside the volcano until it flows and erupts outside the volcano.

Printed in Great Britain
by Amazon

63195563R00031